DON'T TEACH

let me learn about

TEAR - JERKERS
HUMOR
CARTOONS & COMICS
THE NEWSPAPER

by

Nina E. Crosby
Elizabeth H. Marten

To the Teacher:

"Don't Teach! Let Me Learn!" was developed by practicing educators to provide a vehicle for reaching and motivating the intermediate-aged student. Each unit allows the student a wide variety of ways to learn and may be used in total or in part as needed to supplement the regular school curriculum.

The level of difficulty of each individual activity is indicated on the Matrix Chart based on Bloom's Taxonomy of Cognitive Thinking. Activities are also classified by subject area. This will aide you in making choices consistent with your goals and objectives.

Also included for your use are suggestions for record keeping. A student log allows the student to keep records of his progress and provides a means for you to evaluate or assess his progress.

Each unit study contains many activity choices providing stimulation and variation for your students. Activity titles and objectives are identified. Activity language is directed to the student. Activities are complete rather than dependent upon one another, therefore, they may be used to meet your classroom needs.

Illustrations by Zilliox

© 1979
D.O.K. Publishers, Inc.
Buffalo, N.Y. 14214

ISBN NO. 0-914634-61-5

Contents

DON'T TEACH! LET ME LEARN!

"Don't Teach! Let Me Learn!" is a series of multi-disciplinary units of instruction capitalizing on student interest and spotlighting necessary skill development. These units are intended to extend and enrich the elementary school curriculum by broadening the topics and providing experiences to help students become more skillful in interpretation of materials, application of independent study skills and stimulation of creative thinking.

Activities in unit packs may be used as a supplement to regular curriculum. Each unit may be used as a total classroom study or with individual students exhibiting a special interest. Portions of the unit or single activities may be selected to enrich a specific lesson or to extend the work of a single student or group. Likewise, the entire unit may be used for a specialized, intense study on an independent basis.

Nina E. Crosby   Elizabeth H. Marten

LEVEL	GOALS	ACTIVITY DESIGN
Knowledge	Ability to recall facts, concepts or principles.	List, recognize, label, locate, describe, define, observe
Comprehension	Ability to translate or interpret information. A grasp of meaning, intent relationship is demonstrated in oral, written, or non-verbal communication.	Explain, demonstrate, show, paraphrase, experiment, discover, illustrate, infer, predict
Application	Ability to apply previously acquired knowledge or information to a new or concrete situation.	Organize, collect, summarize, order, record, classify, model, construct, relate, generalize, transfer, code, draw, reconstruct.
Analysis	Ability to break down material into its component so that organizational structure may be understood.	Take away, put together, formulate, deduce, compare, contrast, combine, solve, discriminate, take apart, fill in.
Systhesis	Ability to analyze the parts and put them together to form a new whole.	Create, imagine, suppose, predict, assume, translate, hypothesize, design, derive.
Evaluation	Ability to make judgments based on evidence and determine the value of material based on definite criteria.	Appraise, interpret, judge, validate, justify, criticize assess, decide, defend, rate.

Objective Key:

K	—	knowledge
C	—	comprehension
Ap	—	application
An	—	analysis
S	—	synthesis
E	—	evaluation

STUDENT ACTIVITY RECORD

Student: _____

Teacher: _____

Topic: _____

ACTIVITY NUMBER	COMMENTS	OFFICIAL	DATE BEGUN	DATE COMPLETED

D.O.K. Publishers

Tear Jerkers

TEAR-JERKERS

ACTIVITY	Knowledge	Comprehension	Application	Analysis	Synthesis	Evaluation
1				X		X
2		X		X		X
3	X	X		X	X	
4			X	X		X
5	X	X				
6		X			X	X
7	X	X	X		X	
8	X	X	X		X	
9	X			X	X	X
10				X	X	X
11	X		X			
12	X	X	X			
13	X			X		X
14		X	X	X		
15		X	X	X	X	
16		X		X	X	X
17				X	X	
18		X		X		X
19					X	X
20				X	X	X
21			X	X	X	X
22		X			X	X
23					X	X
24		X	X			
25			X		X	
26				X	X	X
27			X	X		
28	X	X	X	X	X	
29	X	X				
30	X	X				

ACTIVITY	Knowledge	Comprehension	Application	Analysis	Synthesis	Evaluation
31		X				
32	X	X				
33	X	X		X	X	X
34	X	X		X	X	
35	X	X				
36	X	X				
37	X	X		X		
38			X			X
39	X	X	X			
40		X				
41		X	X	X		X
42				X	X	X
43		X		X		X
44				X		X
45	X					
46	X		X	X		
47		X	X		X	

1. THE BIRTHDAY PARTY

OBJECTIVE: An, E

It is your brother's or sister's birthday. You
and your family have planned a huge surprise
party, but it is a busy time of the year. Only
two of the invited guests come. How would you
feel? How do you think your brother/sister
would feel? What could you do to make him/
her feel better?

3. GANGSTERS AND GUN MOLLS

OBJECTIVE: K, C, An, S

During the Roaring Twenties, gangsters like Al
Capone and Bonnie and Clyde reigned supreme.
They kept the country in a state of terror.
Present a skit to show the influence of the
gangsters during this time. Who were some
other notorious characters you might want
to include?

5. THE BATTERED CHILD

OBJECTIVE: K, C

Child abuse is a growing concern in the United
States. It is happening in a large number of
families of all kinds. Find out from local
agencies what problems exist in your area and
what is being done to help these children.

2. FAT IS WHERE IT'S AT

OBJECTIVE: C, An, E

We often hear that fat people are jolly. Do you
believe this is so? Give reasons. Now for some
insight into the situation. Pretend that you are
a reporter. You are to interview the Fat Lady in
the circus. Try to organize your questions so
that you get a true picture of her feelings.
What do you think her responses might be?

4. SAD SURVEY

OBJECTIVE: Ap, An, E

Choose 10 things that make you sad. Read your
list to a large number of other students. Have
them tell you which they consider to be the
most sad. Make a graph to show your data. Is
there a difference in what girls consider to
be sad and what boys find sad? If there is a
difference, give reasons that this might be so.

6. SAD MUSIC

OBJECTIVE: C, S, E

Choose some recordings of music that make you
sad. As you listen to the music, draw what
you feel.

7. DISASTER MOVIES

OBJECTIVE: K, C, Ap, S

Disaster movies have been very popular in the
last few years. Examples: Earthquake
                                   The Hindenburg
                                   Towering Inferno
                                   Jaws
Use one of the above topics and create a table
top exhibit or mural depicting scenes.

9. SLAVERY

OBJECTIVE: K, An, S, E

Slavery was abolished in the United States about
110 years ago. There were many sad situations
which existed during this period of our country's
history. Read about the slave ships, slave auc-
tions, work days, and uprooting of families.
Write your reaction to this situation from the
viewpoint of a slave and also the viewpoint of
the master. You might write as a diary or prepare a diorama or T.V. show. You might want to
read about these people to help you FEEL what
they must have been feeling: Frederick Douglas,
Harriet Tubman, Jane Pitman,

11. LITTLE ORPHAN ANNIE

OBJECTIVE: K, Ap

Little Orphan Annie is a very old comic strip.
Trace the evolvement of this character. Read
about the cartoonist.

8. Continued from 7

You might want to research other topics for this activity. Some suggestions are:

Chicago fire   Tsunami
Atom bomb over Hiroshima   Volcanic Eruptions
Gettysburg   La Brea Tar Pits
San Francisco Earthquake   Forest Fires

10. PET DEATH

OBJECTIVE: An, S, E

Pretend your pet dog has died. Choose classmates to be your mother, father, teacher, and best friend. Discuss your feelings with each of them. How does each of these people react to you? Which is the most helpful? Why?

12. ANNIE

OBJECTIVE: K, C, Ap

Annie is a recent Broadway hit. Find the album. Listen to the music. Summarize the story.

13. ORPHANAGES

OBJECTIVE: K, An, E

Research the history of orphanages. How have
they improved over the years? Put yourself
in the orphan's place. How do you think you
would react to institutional living?

15. TEARY SEARCH

OBJECTIVE: C, Ap, An, S

Find and read several stories which bring tears
to your eyes. Why are they so sad? What ele-
ments do stories have which are considered tear
jerkers? Use these components to write your
own sad story.

17. AIRPLANE DOWN

OBJECTIVE: An, S

You have been involved in an airplane crash in
the mountains far away from civilization. Create a skit to show what you would do.

14. AM I REALLY DIFFERENT?

OBJECTIVE: C, Ap, An

Have you ever wondered if YOU were the ONLY one
who felt a certain way or cared about certain
things? Read Are You There God. It's Me,
Margaret. Maybe this will help. Summarize
the story.

16. SURVIVORS

OBJECTIVE C, An, S, E

A severe storm has destroyed your community.
The only survivors are: a 74 year old man;
2 women, ages 26 and 34, a doctor, 3 teenagers, a carpenter, and you. How would
you organize these people to survive?
What jobs would they do? Why? What are
some problems you would face?

18. AUTO ACCIDENT

OBJECTIVE: C, An, E

You and a friend are riding your bikes. A car
comes out of nowhere and hits your friend.
Describe the situation. Tell how you feel.
What would you do? What do others around you
do?

19. EXPLAIN THIS

OBJECTIVE: S, E

Your teacher has made a very important homework assignment for today. You didn't do the assignment. Explain this to your teacher.

21. TOGETHERNESS

OBJECTIVE: Ap, An, S, E

Where the Lillies Bloom is a story that forces children to assume adult roles because of the death of their grandfather and the family's desire to remain together. What problems would you face if you suddenly lost your parents? What would happen to you and your family? Think of other things that might have happened to the family in the story. Write a different ending.

23. POSSESSIONS

OBJECTIVE: S, E

Your house is hit by a tornado. Nearly everything is destroyed. What would be the most difficult thing to replace? What would you try to save? Why?

20. THE THIEF

OBJECTIVE: An, S, E

An article has been stolen in your classroom. You have been unjustly accused. What would your reaction be?

22. TERMINAL ILLNESS

OBJECTIVE: C, S, E

Something for Joey, Brian's Song, Sunshine and Eric are all movies and/or novels with much suffering and sadness because of terminal illness. What is meant by terminal illness? Suppose someone in your family was terminally ill. How would you feel? What could you do to help the person?

24. THE SOAPS

OBJECTIVE: C, Ap

Television soap opera relies heavily on sadness, trouble, and tragedy. Write a soap opera for your class to present.

25. NOW WHAT?

OBJECTIVE: Ap, S

You have lost your brother's catchers mitt or
broken your sister's favorite record album.
Explain the situation to them. Write the
dialogue as it might occur.

27. SAD SACKS

OBJECTIVE: Ap, An

Cartoons and comic strips depict some characters
as losers or continually meeting sad situations.
Examples: Charlie Brown
          Sad Sack
          Mr. Wilson
          Cinderella
Develop a sad character. Place this character
into situtations where he continually loses.

29. TEAR DUCTS

OBJECTIVE: K, C

Why are you crying. Are onions really a sad
vegetable? Is smoke a reason for sadness?
Does black pepper cause sorrow. What really
causes us--physically--to cry? Find out.
Draw a diagram to explain the working of
the eye in relation to tears.

26. SECOND STRINGER

OBJECTIVE: An, S, E

Your school is forming a softball team. Every-
one knows that only 20 players will be selected
for the team. You really want to play. When
the list is posted, your name is not on it.
What do you do? How do you feel? How would
you react to your best friend, who was chosen?

28. TRAIL OF TEARS

OBJECTIVE: K, C, Ap, An, S

The Trail of Tears is a factual event. It relates
to the history of the American Indians and their
relocation. Research this trail. Show on a map,
its route.
Write a diary from the viewpoint of an Indian
child on their daily trek.
Relate experiences and feelings.
Write an editorial (or draw an editorial cartoon) dealing with this subject. Decide on a
caption.

30. A VISIT TO THE HOSPITAL

OBJECTIVE: K, C

Visiting the hospital--as a patient--can be a
frightening experience. Call local hospitals
and/or pediatricians to discover what is being
done to prepare young people for hospital stays.
Ask for literature. Prepare a report for your
class.

31. DENTIST PHOBIA

OBJECTIVE: C

Prepare a skit showing a scary visit to the dentist's office. Show fear. Reverse the visit. Show what could have been done to prevent this fear.

33. ACCIDENTS DO HAPPEN

OBJECTIVE: K, C, An, S, E

Our senses are very important to us. However, some people via accident or birth defect, do not have their sense of hearing or sight. If you had to give up one of these, which would you be able to lose most easily. Why did you make this choice? Find out about organizations which help the handicapped. Read about them. Prepare a report for your group. You might want to read: Follow My Leader, Helen Keller, Child of the Silent Night.

35. FAIRY TALES

OBJECTIVE: K, C

Many times, in fairy tales, something tragic or violent happened to the main character. However, they usually "lived happily ever after". Think of examples: witches, poison apples, locked in towers, etc. Using some of these situations, write an original fairy tale. Illustrate it. Does it end "happily ever after"?

32. SCOLIOSIS

OBJECTIVE: K, Ap

What is being done in your community for scoliosis? Ask your school nurse for an expla-
nation of scoliosis and its check-ups and
treatment. Orthopedists are doctors who treat
this spinal problem. Call them for information
and pamphlets. Prepare a display. There may
be a Scoliosis Organization in your area.
They would help you. Get your classmates
informed.

34. COULD THIS HAPPEN AGAIN?

OBJECTIVE: K, C, An, S

Have you read The Diary of Ann Frank? Or View
From the Attic? Both of these are real life
experiences as related from a young Jewish girl's
viewpoint during World War II in Nazi Germany.
Read about the plight of Jews at this time. Compare this to the situation in Ireland and South
Africa today. What parellels can you draw, if
any? Use newspapers, news magazines and broad-
casts to help you.

36. MARTYRDOM

OBJECTIVE, K, C

There have been martyrs, saints and political
victims in the history of our world. These
people have believed in a cause to the point
where their lives were lost in its defense.
Explain the meaning of Martyr, Martyrdom,
Saint, Saint hood

37. FAMOUS MARTYRS, SAINTS AND POLITICAL VICTIMS

OBJECTIVE: K, C, An

Research these people. Tell what happened to
them. In your report, tell about their beliefs
which led to persecution and/or death.
Examples: Joan of Arc, Martin Luther King, Jr.,
          Jesus Christ, Czar Nicholas II,
          Nathan Hale
How would you classify these people. Martyr?
Saint? Political victim?

39. VIOLENCE IN NURSERY RHYMES

OBJECTIVE: K, C, Ap

Horror stories at bedtime? Even the most well-
known rhymes and tales had sadness. For
INSTANCE: Humpty Dumpty fell off a wall!
          Miss Muffett was scared!
          Jill fell down a hill!
List as many other examples as you can from
childhood rhymes which deal with fear, accidents or tragedy.

41. IT MAKES ME SAD

OBJECTIVE: C, Ap, An, E

Think of something that has happened to you that
made you very sad. Write an original story to
explain the situation.

38. THE FIRST DAY

OBJECTIVE: An, E

Your father has been transferred because of his
job. Your family has had to move to a new city
during the summer vacation. It is time for
school to start. Describe your feelings on
that first day in a new school. How do other
people make you feel?

40. SAD SITUATIONS

OBJECTIVE: Ap

Act out these sad situations:
    -- a plant during a drought
    -- a broken Easter egg
    -- worn out tires on ice and snow
    -- a pencil being sharpened
    -- an insect caught in a spider web
Think of others of your own.

42. DEAR ABBY

OBJECTIVE: An, S, E

Make a "Dear Abby" box for your classroom. Have
classmates write letters about their problems
for the box. Select some of these letters to
discuss with the class. Try to find as many
solutions as possible to help correct the
situation.

43. SAD COLORS

OBJECTIVE: C, An, E

Colors affect our thinking and actions. Think
about color and how it affects you. Make self-
portraits using color to show sadness, anger,
loneliness and grief.

45. KIDNAPPED

OBJECTIVE: K

When aviator Charles Lindbergh's baby was kidnapped
the entire United States was shocked and saddened.
Research this famous kidnapping. Give the circum-
stances. Tell about the family. What was the
final outcome? Can you identify other well-known
situations involving kidnapping.

47. SAD COMMERCIALS

OBJECTIVE: C, Ap, S

Rejection makes us sad. Television commercials
sometimes use rejection to sell a product. Remember the fellow who never had a date because
he had bad breath? Or the heartbreak of psori-
asis? Can you think of other examples? Write
a television commercial of your own using
rejection to sell your product.

44. DADDYS DON'T CRY

OBJECTIVE: An, E

How does it make you feel to see others cry?
What kinds of feelings do you have when your
best friend cries? Your mother? Your father?
Why do we usually associate tears with girls
and women? Why is it considered unmanly to
cry? Is this true in all cultures?

46. SAVE THE CHILDREN

OBJECTIVE: K, Ap, An

SAVE THE CHILDREN is an organization that ad-
vertises in current magazines and on television in an attempt to provide help for the
world's underprivileged children. Make a collection of photographs used by this organization. Why do you think these pictures are
selected? What emotions do they invoke? How
do the pictures make you feel? Find out about
this organization. What does it do?

Humor

HUMOR

ACTIVITY	Knowledge	Comprehension	Application	Analysis	Synthesis	Evaluation
1			X			
2	X			X	X	
3		X	X	X		X
4	X			X		X
5				X	X	
6				X		X
7	X			X		X
8		X	X			
9		X			X	
10		X			X	
11			X		X	
12			X		X	
13		X	X			
14	X	X				
15	X				X	
16					X	
17	X				X	
18		X	X			
19		X			X	
20		X	X			
21				X	X	X
22				X	X	X
23				X	X	
24				X	X	
25		X				
26		X				
27				X	X	
28			X	X	X	
29		X			X	
30		X			X	

ACTIVITY	Knowledge	Comprehension	Application	Analysis	Synthesis	Evaluation
31	X			X	X	
32	X			X	X	
33	X			X	X	
34	X	X	X			
35	X		X	X		
36		X	X	X		
37					X	X
38					X	
39					X	
40				X	X	X
41			X	X		X
42	X			X	X	
43			X		X	X
44			X		X	X
45		X			X	
46		X			X	
47				X	X	
48			X	X		
49					X	
50			X	X		X
51				X	X	
52				X		X
53			X			
54	X	X		X		X
55	X			X		
56	X		X			
57		X			X	
58		X			X	
59		X				
60	X			X	X	

1. JOKE BOOK

OBJECTIVE: Ap

Make a collection of jokes. Organize them in a Good Humor Book. You may want to arrange them in categories and illustrate them.

---

3. COLLOQUIAL HUMOR

OBJECTIVE: C, Ap, An, E

What people in one part of the country think is funny, other cultures do not. What is meant by colloquialisms? Do you understand these? "tacky", "over yonder", "ret up your closet", "please?" These are colloquial expressions. Can you think of colloquial expressions from your area that others might find strange or humorous? What phrases have you heard from other areas of the country or world that are amusing to you?

---

5. MIME

OBJECTIVE: An, S

Cantiflas of Mexico and Harpo Marx of the Marx Brothers were great mime artists. Think of a funny story that you know (or make up one). Tell the story to the class as a pantomime. See if you can make the story understood and appreciated with no words.

2. SLAPSTICK

OBJECTIVE: K, An, S

Charlie Chaplin, Laurel and Hardy, and Red Skelton are considered slapstick comedians. Their humor has been enjoyed for many years. What is slapstick? View films of these comedians. Tell why they are funny. What makes the humor last through time? Plan your own slapstick routine.

4. PLAYS

OBJECTIVE: K, An, E

Shakespeare wrote a number of plays. Some were tragedies, others were historical, and still others were classified as comedies. Read several different Shakespearean stories representing each type. Tell why the plays called comedies are classified this way. Pick out parts of the story that you consider to be funny.

6. FUNNY FLICKS

OBJECTIVE: An, E

Choose two funny movies you have seen. Tell how they were alike and how they were different. Tell what made each funny to you. How could each have been improved?

7. STEREOTYPING

OBJECTIVE: K, An, E

What is a stereotype? Consider the kinds of
ethnic humor that exist. Give a summary of
the stereotype the humor implies for each
group you identified.

9. SILLY SYLLOGISMS

OBJECTIVE: C, S

If your reasoning is faulty or you start with a
false statement or you let your feelings affect
your judgement, you will end up with a silly
syllogism.

Examples: Whales have warm blood.
            I have warm blood.
            Therefore, I am a whale.

11. VAUDEVILLE

OBJECTIVE: Ap, S

Song and dance routines were a major part of
Vaudeville shows. Soft shoe routines were
common. Ted Lewis' top hat and cane will always be remembered. Develop your own soft
shoe number to the music of "Me and My Shadow".
You will probably want a classmate to work with
you.

8. ETHNIC HUMOR

OBJECTIVE: C, Ap

Polish jokes have had wide popularity for a number of years. Archie Bunker in <u>All in the Family</u> uses the Polish as a source of humor. Bill Cosby bases his humor on the Black American. Find examples of humor and jokes that are based on a particular race or culture.

10. Continued from 9

Examples: All comedies are great.
This movie is a comedy.
Therefore, it's certain to be great.

Jane and Joan are in a contest.
I like Jane the best.
Therefore, Jane will probably win.

Make up several syllogisms on your own. Do a reversal. Make several sensible ones on your own.

12. KIDS AND COMEDY

OBJECTIVE: Ap, S

The Bowery Boys, The Little Rascals, Dennis the Menace, and the Brady Bunch are examples of humorous shows based on the actions or activities of children. Write a funny story about kids. Watch a young child or a group of young children for ideas. Perhaps you will get ideas from younger brothers and sisters.

13. SMILE EXPERIMENT

OBJECTIVE: C, Ap

As you go about your regular day, SMILE! Keep a
record of the number of people who greeted you,
in return, with a smile. Likewise, how many
did not?

15. SYNONYMS AND ANTONYMS

OBJECTIVE: K, S

See how many words are synonyms for laugh. Use
your thesaurus. Would you be able to use all of
these in a funny story? Try.

Do a reversal. Find antonyms for laugh. Sometimes, things can be so tragic they become a
comedy of errors. Can you accomplish a comedy
or errors in story form?

17. SMILE MEDLEY

OBJECTIVE: K, S

See how many records you can get that relate to
happiness. Find out what is meant by a medley.
Prepare a taped medley of these songs and play
for your group. Remember--a medley should flow
from one piece to another!

14. "SMILE AND THE WORLD SMILES WITH YOU"

OBJECTIVE: K, C

"Smile and the World Smiles With You", Let a
Smile be Your Umbrella", "Happy Talk"--These
are all phrases which denote happiness and
smiling. Make a collection of song titles
or phrases which have something to do with
this theme.

16. WEAR A HAPPY FACE!

OBJECTIVE: S

        Smile buttons were being worn and sold
a few years ago. They were bright yellow with
black eyes and smiling mouth. Today, there are
all kinds of buttons with funny pictures and
catchy sayings. Design your own funny buttons.

18. BE ON THE LOOK OUT!

OBJECTIVE: C, Ap

Be on the look out for funny phrases, sayings,
words, looks, etc. Look in cartoons, comic
strips, comic books and magazines. Make a collection of the varied ways an author has to
show us something is funny. After cutting out,
make an interesting collage with your collection.

19. HUMOROUS POSTERS

OBJECTIVE: C, S

Posters are also being published with phrases
and funny sayings and pictures. Prepare some
to brighten your room or school. Be sure to
think about color, balance, design and let-
tering.

21. CLASS PROPHESY

OBJECTIVE: An, S, E

First, what is a prophesy? Create a situation
where you are looking into the future, seeing
your classmates as they are (teacher too),
THEN--Knowing them as you presently do--their
strengths, weaknesses, interests, personality,
etc., what do you predict for them for the
future? Sometimes, it is funnier to write
opposites rather than attempt to place them
where you actually think they'll be. (over)

23. SILLY SONGS

OBJECTIVE: An, S

Songs which are silly to one person may not seem
silly to others, so none are listed here. Can you
think of present day songs which you consider
silly? If you can find the record, play it for
your class. Do they agree? What makes it silly?
Ask your parents or grandparents for silly song
titles from their era.

20. PHOTO FUN

OEJECTIVE: C, Ap

Take a camera walk around your school. Snap
funny scenes happening before your very eyes.
When the pictures return, arrange for the whole
school to see "What's Happening That's Funny".
Add interesting and clever captions for the
pictures. Perhaps you will want to add music,
too.

22. Continued from 21

Have a setting from which you're predicting.
Even though you will be talking about indivi-
duals, have a story theme to tie them all together. Take it all in fun! After all, who
can really predict? Is there anyone? What
do you predict for yourself? How and why
can you make these predictions.

24. Continued from 23

If you're lucky, maybe old records exist at home
or at the public library. Two of MY all time
favorites are "Aba Daba Honeymoon" (Would you
believe?) and "Mare's Eat Oats and Does Eat
Oats" (say this fast for the silly effect!)
Why don't you try making up your own silly
song? Use a well known tune and add your own
words or--try words and music.

25. CAN YOU TOP THIS?

OBJECTIVE: C

Stories get bigger and bigger as one person tries
to top another. Tall Tales result, like Paul Bun-
yon or John Henry. Read Carl Sandburg's <u>Tornado</u>.
How many phrases get bigger and bigger---really
exaggerated? List them. Try some of your own.
Use these to get you started:

    as big as_____
    as fast as_____
    as tiny as_____

27. JOKES, LIMERICKS, RIDDLES

OBJECTIVE: An, S

Put together a Fun Reader. Collect favorite
jokes, limericks, and riddles. Share the
booklet with others. Illustrations would
make it better.

Take a close look at limericks. Figure out
the pattern. Write your own limericks.

29. PYRAMID POETRY

OBJECTIVE: C, S

Pyramid Poetry can be done like a riddle also.
First construct a pyramid from cardboard. Be
careful to measure closely and correctly. Use
this form as a pyramid riddle for each side of
the pyramid.

                    Noun
             adjective, adjective
        participle, participle, participle
Statement about but which does not identify the topic
        Answer: Inside or on bottom of pyramid

(over)

26. Continued from 25

        as pretty as_____
        as long as_____
        as mean as_____
Can you think of others? Put these into complete
sentences. Try to use as many as you can in cre-
ating your own tall tale. Can you think of an interesting way to write your tall tale? How could
it be displayed to show that it is a tall tale--
an exaggeration?

28. RIDDLES

OBJECTIVE: Ap, An, S

Is there a writing pattern to riddles? Try
writing riddles about classmates. Read orally
and let the class guess who you are talking
about.

30. Continued from 29

Example:

                    Friend
            furry   intelligent
        helping leading protecting
        Eyes and ears for man
                Who am I?

            Seeing eye dog

36

31. KEEP TALKING

OBJECTIVE: K, An, S

This can be an entire class activity or a group. The idea is: One person begins a story (original) and continues talking until the leader claps his hands. When the hands are clapped, the next person picks up the story, at that point (even in the middle of a word perhaps). He must then continue the story. He must be a good listener to know what has already happened. (over)

33. HUMOR PROPS

OBJECTIVE: K, An, S

In the world of theater props, objects have various uses. What are props? Look at home for interesting props: old hats, boots, fishing poles, brooms, etc. Bring them to school. Place in a box or grab bag. See if you and your classmates can think on your feet. Individually, each member of the class chooses one of the props. They use this prop, without prior preparation, to act out or talk about a situation with its use. The more absurd stories, the better. Let your imagination fly!

35. BE A CLOWN

OBJECTIVE: K, Ap, An

Kelly is one of the most famous clowns in the world. Did you know there is actually a school for clowns? Read about it. Tell about its curriculum.

32. Continued from 31

This continues until all have had their turn.
The time allotted for each person can vary.
It can be extremely short or perhaps several
minutes long. The idea is to keep the story
moving at a fast pace. Listen to see how
many different turns the story will take!

34. VENTRILOQUISM

OBJECTIVE: K, C, Ap

Edgar Bergen and Charlie McCarthy were a team.
Paul Winchell has his partners. One of these
was a very "smart dummy". Who was the dummy?
Ventriloquism is quite an art. Get books from
your library or toy departments. Find out the
techniques used and see what you can do. Try
to refashion an old doll or toy to work for you.
It might be fun to make up your own show having
a "dummy". Perhaps your "dummy" might be another classmate who can work for you. This will
take practice and coordination.

36. CLOWN FACES

OBJECTIVE: Ap, An, S

In Childcraft, there is a section written about
clown make-ups. Read about this and design your
own clown face. Remember, this should be your
original design. Practice with facial drawings
before reacing your decision.

37. CLOWN CLOTHES

OBJECTIVE: S, E

Design and illustrate your own personal preference for your clown outfit. This should fit the
type clown you intend to be. How do clown out-
fits reflect the clown "personality"?

39. STAND UP COMEDIAN!

OBJECTIVE: S

Some comics work with other people. Some work
alone on stage. Before they go on, however,
much work and practice goes into their routine.
Joke writers are employed to add to their material.
Find your own joke writers or be one yourself.
You can "borrow" jokes which have already been
written, but try to come up with your own. Put
together your own stand-up routine. Try it, on
your own, for your class.

41. THE FUNNIEST COMIC TODAY

OBJECTIVE: Ap, An, E

Who do you consider to be the funniest comic of
today? Write an essay about this person giving
your reasons. Cite examples of this person's
humor.

38. BE A CLOWN, TOO

OBJECTIVE: S

Get together a group of classroom clowns. Prepare your own routine. Try adding tumbling, gymnastics, or juggling to your act. Have fun!

40. WHAT IF?

OBJECTIVE: An, S, E

What if our nose was on top of our head?
What if our feet grew from our wrists?
What if a dog had wings?
What if we had eyes on our shoulder blades?
What problems might arise from these situations?
What alterations would we have to make? What changes in our life would this cause? What would become new necessities? Speculate!!
On changes!! On new problems!! On new advantages!!

42. VOCABULARY

OBJECTIVE: K, S, E

Write the meaning of these words:

laugh	guffaw	chuckles	chortle
comedian	snicker	giggle	cartoon
humor	levity		

Demonstrate the different kinds of laughs from this list.

43. PROFESSIONAL LAUGHER

OBJECTIVE: Ap, S, E

How would you like to be paid to laugh on cue?
There actually are people who are being paid to
do just that. T.V. comedy shows have them
placed in their audiences and THEIR laughter
causes others to laugh. Do you know people who
have infectious laughs?   (over)

—

45. TOM SWIFTIES

OBJECTIVE: C, S

I'll dig you later", Tom said gravely.
"Don't be chicken", he said fouly.
"These hot dogs are good", Tom said frankly.
These are examples of Tom Swifties. Make Tom
Swifties of your own. Now try some occupa-
tional Tom Swifties.

—

47. KINDS OF LAUGHS

OBJECTIVE: An, S

List qualities of laughter which make some laughs
better than others. Can you give them names?
Can you make up new names for particular laughs?
Example: Guffaw, chortle, belly popper

44. Continued from 43

People who, by laughing, cause you and others to
laugh? Take your tape recorder and record these
great "laughers". Find them at school, at home,
anywhere you go. Play your tape for your class
or group. Did any of the laughers cause your
group to laugh? You might want to evaluate each
laugh on a scale of 1-5. Compare the scores.
Was there one laugh which was the favorite.

46. Continued from 45

Examples: "You must have a shot", the doctor
said sharply.
"I love to sleep outdoors," said the
hunter intently.
Here are some modifiers to help you get started.

thinly	silently	brightly	cuttingly
pointedly	dryly	fouly	swiftlessly
blindly	craftily	hotly	crisply
crustily	painfully	piercingly	foggily
pitifully	frostily		

48. THAT'S THE SITUATION

OBJECTIVE: Ap, An

What is situation comedy? Write a skit that
might be considered situation comedy. Perhaps
you will want to present it to the class.

49. BE A CARTOONIST

OBJECTIVE: S

Draw your own original cartoon and give it a
caption. Try it out on your friends to find
out if it is really funny.

51. HUMOROUS ESSAY

OBJECTIVE: An, S

Write an essay on the most humorous thing you
have ever had happen to you.

53. GRAPHING A LAUGH

OBJECTIVE: Ap

Choose two of your favorite jokes. Try them on
various people. Graph your results as to which
joke people believed to be the funniest.

50. WRITE A LETTER

OBJECTIVE: Ap, An, E

Write a personal letter to a favorite comedian.
Tell why you enjoy this person's humor, and
what you like best to see them do. Use correct letter form.

52. WHAT IS FUNNY?

OBJECTIVE: An, E

What makes things funny? Evaluate stories, cartoons, and television comedy. Make a list of
things that are funny. Try to determine why
they are funny.

54. THE HUMORIST

OBJECTIVE: K, C, An, E

Will Rogers was considered a humorist. Read
about him. Why was he considered a humorist?
Would Bob Hope be considered a humorist? Give
reasons.

55. EDITORIAL HUMOR

OBJECTIVE: K, S

Find out what an editorial cartoon is. Write an editorial cartoon, with humor, about a present happening at school or in the "news".

—

57. CAREER CHOICE

OBJECTIVE: Ap, S

Career choice completions can be interesting. Complete each with a humorous reason:

Examples: I could have been a lawyer, but I'm not allowed to argue.
I could have been a pilot, but I don't have wings.

—

59. NURSERY RHYME FUN

OBJECTIVE: Ap

Just for fun, think about your favorite nursery rhymes. Design a new "tuffet" for Miss Muffet, or something else for Little Jack Horner to pull out of the pie. Write your own original verses.

56. GREEK COMEDY

OBJECTIVE: K, An

In Greek drama, there were two masks--one for comedy, one for tragedy. What did the masks look like? How were Greek tragedies and comedies different?

58. Continued from 57

Now try these:

I could have been a carpenter, but_____
I could have been a teacher, but_____
I could have been a policeman, but_____
I could have been a politician, but_____
I could have been a nurse, but_____

60. FUNNY PICTURES

OBJECTIVE: K, An, S

Caricatures are funny and interesting. Find out what caricatures are. Draw caricatures of your classmates, your teacher and yourself.

SOME OF OUR OWN IDEAS:

Cartoons and Comics

CARTOONS & COMIC STRIPS

ACTIVITY	Knowledge	Comprehension	Application	Analysis	Synthesis	Evaluation
1		X	X		X	
2	X	X	X		X	
3	X	X	X		X	
4		X	X		X	
5		X	X		X	
6	X	X	X		X	
7		X		X	X	
8		X	X	X	X	
9	X	X		X		X
10		X		X	X	
11		X		X	X	
12	X	X	X		X	
13	X					X
14	X		X	X		X
15	X		X	X		X
16				X	X	X
17				X	X	X
18				X	X	X
19		X	X	X		
20	X	X		X		X
21	X	X	X		X	
22	X		X	X		
23		X	X	X		X
24		X	X		X	
25		X	X	X	X	
26		X	X	X	X	
27		X	X	X	X	
28	X	X		X	X	
29		X	X	X	X	
30		X	X	X	X	X

ACTIVITY	Knowledge	Comprehension	Application	Analysis	Synthesis	Evaluation
31		X	X			
32		X	X	X	X	X
33		X	X	X	X	X
34	X					X
35	X			X		
36		X	X		X	

1. PIXWORDS

OBJECTIVE: C, Ap, S

These are words which contain a picture that denotes the meaning of the word. Examples:

bómb! rain

3. QUOTOPIX

OBJECTIVE: K, C, Ap, S

These words name famous people and contain drawings which relate to their accomplishments.

Example: Betsy Ross   FRANKLIN

Can you think of others?

5. WORDLES

OBJECTIVE: C, Ap, S

A wordle is commonly found in newspapers and magazines. They express meaning by the shape and placement of letters.

Example: LAWYER (crooked lawyer)
         SPY (undercover spy)

Wordle away!

2. INVENTOPIX

OBJECTIVE: K, C, Ap, S

These are words which are the name of an inventor and are written to look like, include or represent the invention. Example:

FULT☉N   EDIS☉N

Make as many inventopix as you can.

4. DROODLES

OBJECTIVE: C, Ap, S

Droodles are great fun and really challenge your imagination. They do not have to make sense to be funny. Example:

A DOGWOOD TREE   DONUT REJECT

Draw your droodles.

6. HOMOPHIX

OBJECTIVE: K, C, Ap, S

Using homonyms, pair them in a funny way.
Example:

 plain-plane    bored-board

Can you think of homophix?

7. NEW WORD CARTOONS

OBJECTIVE: C, An, S

Can you create original word cartoons of your own? What about animalpix or antonympix?

9. WHAT IS IT?

OBJECTIVE: K, C, An, E

Find out what editorializing means. Look in local newspapers, news magazines, etc. to find examples of editorial cartoons. Explain the meaning and its relevancy to today's world.

11. EDITORIAL POSTER

OBJECTIVE: C, An, S

Prepare a poster for your class or school which is an editorial cartoon. Use a pressing class or school problem.
Examples: Debris in the lunchroom
             Dismissal time
             Free time

8. NEW IMPROVED DICTIONARY

OBJECTIVE: C, Ap, An, S

Create a new word. Illustrate its meaning.
Write its meaning. Perhaps you will want to
make a dictionary of your new words with
illustrations and meanings.

10. LISTEN AND DRAW

OBJECTIVE: C, An, S

After reading or listening to local, state or
national news, draw and caption an editorial
cartoon.

12. EDITORIAL BIRTHDAY GREETING

OBJECTIVE: K, C, Ap, S

Draw an editorial cartoon as a birthday message.
Write an accompanying verse. Direct it to a famous person expressing your feelings about a
recent decision he has made.

Examples: President of the United States
          School Board
          T.V. Personality

13. PERSUASION

OBJECTIVE: K, E

Editorial cartoons serve several purposes. Often, they are used to help persuade people. Make a list of vocabulary words which might be used to help persuade. Give your reasons why these words might be considered to be persuasion words.

15. REACH A CONCLUSION

OBJECTIVE: K, Ap, An, E

In a small group, decide upon the groups' three favorite cartoons or comic strips which have been seen for many years. Examples: Orphan Annie, Superman, Batman, Popeye, Dick Tracy, etc. Analyze why these cartoons and comic strips have endured for so many years. List your reasons. Present your information to the other class groups. Were all groups in agreement? Does anyone disagree with the reasons given?

17. CHARACTERISTICS

OBJECTIVE: An, S, E

Some well known comic strip characters come into contact with villainous people. What characteristics might a villain possess?

14. IDENTIFY YOUR FAVORITES

OBJECTIVE: K, Ap, An, E

Choose your five favorite comic strips. List them in order of preference. Tell which characters and situations you like best about each one. Give your reasons for your choices. Do they fall into any category or are all of them the same type?

16. COLORS

OBJECTIVE: An, S, E

Colors are used in comic strips and cartoons on T.V. to create images and feelings. Choose the color which you feel would best represent the following:

- a. jealousy
- b. envy
- c. happiness
- d. strength
- e. fury
- f. heat
- g. cold
- h. sadness
- i. peace
- j. sickness

Go on with your "senses". What do the above smell like? feel like? taste like? Put it all together in verse. Illustrate it.

18. SOMETIMES, YES   SOMETIMES, NO

OBJECTIVE: An, S, E

Explain situations where a villian and the hero might be the same person. Give examples.

19. DO IT YOURSELF

OBJECTIVE: C, Ap, An

Create your own villian. Describe his physical,
mental and personality traits. Read your description to others. Have them illustrate from
your description. Did they see what you see?

---

21. OCCUPATIONAL CARTOONS

OBJECTIVE: K, C, Ap, S

Various occupations can be used to create enter-
taining cartoons. These have been referred to
as occupational gramblers. Make up some of your
own and illustrate as a cartoon. Try these:

"That was a close shave," said the barber.
"That is a real horror story," said Dr.
 Frankenstein.
"Do you believe that?" said Mr. Guinness.

---

23. AND HERE HE/SHE IS__

OBJECTIVE: C, Ap, An, E

Develop your own comic strip hero or heroine.
Describe their physical, mental, and personality attributes. Illustrate your character.
It might be fun to read your description to
other class members and have them illustrate
from your reading. Did they see what you see?

20. HEROS/HEROINES

OBJECTIVE: K, C, An, E

What is a hero? How is he different from a heroine? List the characteristics which both
might have. Name as many comic strip or cartoon heros and heroines as you can. Choose
5 of these. What characteristics do they have
in common? How are they different?

22. INANIMATE OBJECTS

OBJECTIVE: K, Ap, An

What is personification? Use every day objects
to create your own comic strip with inanimate
object characters. Put them into normal situations (for them). How do they react to each
other? What do they feel? What do they say?
Why do the same situations look differently
to the different objects? Develop their personality via the comic strip route.

24. SUPER COMIC

OBJECTIVE: C, Ap, S

Place your hero/heroine in an original comic
strip. Make the adventure support the role
of the character.

25. CARTOON BALLOONS

OBJECTIVE: C, Ap, An, S

Balloons are the little enclosures used with
dialogues or thoughts in cartoons and comic
strips. Choose various pictures of cartoons
and comic strips, then provide new thoughts
or new dialogue which would be appropriate
for the action.

27. CARICATURES

OBJECTIVE: C, Ap, An, S

Caricatures are exaggerations. Exaggerations
in physical characteristics as well as personality. Find examples of caricatures. Draw
your own self caricature.

29. BABY PICTURE CARTOONS

OBJECTIVE: C, Ap, An, S

Collect baby pictures from the class. Caption
these after studying the baby's expression.

26. EXAMINING DIALOGUE

OBJECTIVE: C, Ap, An, S

Collect a weeks' examples of one comic strip (a week of Snoopy, for example). Were any phrases often repeated? What statements were used which show the characters' personality? Has a new character been introduced? What do you think this new character will be like in future strips?

28. ANIMAL TRAITS

OBJECTIVE: K, C, An, S

Think about exaggerations in relation to the following ideas. What animal characteristics might a person be given who--
    eats a lot----   is a great runner----
    talks a lot---   has freckles----
    tells tall tales----   laughs loudly----
    is a great swimmer----
Add others of your own.

30. BABY DIALOGUE

OBJECTIVE: C, Ap, An, S, E

Using various baby pictures from your class and teachers, use the pictures in pairs. Write dialogue which would be appropriate for these known characters.

31. SPECIAL BALLOONS

OBJECTIVE: C, Ap

Find examples of balloons which show: anger, fear, noise, or other sounds, sadness, happiness, etc. Make a display of Emotion Balloons, Sound Balloons, etc.

33. IF IT HAD BEEN ME

OBJECTIVE: C, Ap, An, S, E

The comics are full of super heros: Superman, Wonder Woman, Batman, Flash Gordon, and many others. Choose one of these super heros. Pretend that you are that super hero. How would you change the world? Maybe you would want to create a new super hero for yourself.

35. PEANUTS!

OBJECTIVE: K, An

Charles Schultz, the cartoonist of Peanuts fame, is probably the best known modern cartoonist. Find examples of some of his EARLY work. How are these cartoons like the Peanuts characters? How are they different? Schultz had led an interesting life. Write a biography. Discuss his feelings about school in particular.

32. FUNNY YOU

OBJECTIVE: C, Ap, An, S, E

Draw a cartoon or comic strip about the funniest thing that ever happened to you. Write a caption or dialogue for it.

34. DISNEY

OBJECTIVE: K, E

Walt Disney is widely known for his animated cartoons. What is ANIMATION? Write a biography of Disney. Show examples of his work. Why do you think he is an important American cartoonist?

36. ON FILM!

OBJECTIVE: C, Ap, S

Draw your own cartoon or comic strip series. It should be done on paper first so that you can make corrections and changes. Now put your drawings on film for a filmstrip and also make a tape for the story lines. You may find suggestions in Childcraft.

SOME OF OUR OWN IDEAS:

d.o.k.
—

—

d.o.k.
—

—
d.o.k

The Newspaper

THE NEWSPAPER

ACTIVITY	Knowledge	Comprehension	Application	Analysis	Synthesis	Evaluation
1	X	X				
2		X				
3	X	X				
4	X	X				
5	X			X		X
6				X	X	X
7				X		X
8		X	X			
9	X	X				
10		X	X			
11	X			X		
12	X	X	X			
13				X		X
14	X	X		X		
15		X	X			
16	X			X	X	
17	X	X		X		
18			X			
19			X			
20			X			
21	X	X	X			
22				X	X	
23			X	X	X	
24			X	X	X	
25	X		X			
26				X	X	
27			X		X	
28			X		X	X
29			X		X	
30	X					

ACTIVITY	Knowledge	Comprehension	Application	Analysis	Synthesis	Evaluation
31	X	X				
32				X	X	X
33	X					
34		X				
35			X	X		
36		X				
37		X				
38				X		
39	X		X	X		
40			X		X	
41			X		X	
42	X	X				
43		X			X	
44	X					
45			X	X		
46		X	X			
47			X			X
48			X			X
49			X			X
50			X			
51		X	X			
52	X	X		X		
53	X	X	X			
54	X	X	X			
55	X	X	X			
56	X	X	X			
57				X	X	X
58				X	X	X
59	X			X	X	X
60	X			X	X	X

1. NURSERY NEWS

OBJECTIVE: K, C

Rewrite a news story with a base from one of the
fairy tales or nursery rhymes you liked as a
young child.

3. NEWS SCRAPBOOK

OBJECTIVE K, C

Make a scrapbook to show examples of the following newspaper terms and ideas:
a. headline, lead, flag, major news story, dateline, index, ears, and other terms you identify.
b. clip examples of kinds of news stories that
inform, advise, and entertain.
c. clip examples of news that is international,
national and local.

5. EDITORIALS

OBJECTIVE: K, AN, E

Find in your newspaper, two or more editorials
illustrating each of the three functions of
editorials to inform, entertain, to influence. Write your comments concerning the
methods used to accomplish the purpose of
the editorials. How successfully do you
think the authors accomplish their purpose?

2. NEWSROOM DRAMA

OBJECTIVE: C

Follow the series on television called Lou Grant, or watch for Lou Grant's role in the Mary Tyler Moore Show. What information does this give you about news reporting?

4. LIBEL

OBJECTIVE: K, C

Find out what libel means. Give examples.

6. MORE EDITORIALS

OBJECTIVE: An, S, E

Write an editorial about some issue in your school that you and/or others feel strongly about. Perhaps you could write two editorials giving both points of view.

7. AND THEN WHAT?

OBJECTIVE: An, E

Trace the coverage of an important local news story. Was the coverage complete? Were there background stories in addition to "hard news"? Was the treatment of this story fair?

9. DID YOU KNOW?

OBJECTIVE: K, C

Can you answer these questions about newspapers and news writing?
a. How is the newspaper an important part of our daily lives?
b. Do newspapers provide both fact and fiction?
c. What stories do you usually see on the front page?
d. What is a "hard news" story?
e. What are the five W's in newspaper reporting?

11. KINDS OF NEWS

OBJECTIVE: K, An

Collect clippings from each issue of the newspaper to show how it performs its various functions: to inform, to entertain, to persuade. How is each different?

8. BE A REPORTER

OBJECTIVE: C, Ap

Write a news story of your own. Choose something happening at school or in your community. Use the correct writing style.

10. EQUAL TIME:

OBJECTIVE: C, Ap

Do most newspapers try to give equal coverage to all candidates for public office and both sides in a dispute or argument? Give examples of this found in your local newspaper.

12. I BELIEVE

OBJECTIVE: K, C, Ap

The newspaper tries to help the reader decide the meaning of the news by giving its interpretation. Which page of the newspaper is used to state the paper's opinion or interpretation? Show examples to prove your answer.

13. LETTERS, WE GET LETTERS

OBJECTIVE: An, E

How can you or your parents tell a newspaper
your feelings about something? Do you have
strong feelings about a local story or issue?
Let your newspaper know.

15. LEADS

OBJECTIVE, C, Ap

In structuring a news story, the lead paragraph
gives a summary of the event. In one or two
sentences the reader is told who, what, when,
where and why of the story. Write a lead for
a news release about the awakening of Snow
White or the marriage of Cinderella.

17. THE CLASSIFIEDS

OBJECTIVE: K, C, An

How many different kinds of ads can you find in
the classified section? How are these catero-
ries arranged in your local paper? Can you
think of reasons for this arrangement?

14. THE LAW AND THE PRESS

OBJECTIVE: K, C, An

What amendment of the United States Constitution gives protection to the press? State it in your own words. Why is this an important law for the United States citizen? Is this true in all countries? If no, give examples.

16. BY WHO?

OBJECTIVE: K, An, S

What is a news by-line? Do all stories have by-lines? Why? When is a by-line used? Find out from your local paper. Study the by-lines in your newspaper for one week. Does the name of one person show up more than others? From the articles by the leading person, what could you tell about the writer?

18. CLASSIFIED ADS

OBJECTIVE: Ap

Write a real estate ad advertising your home for sale. Describe it well. Keep them guessing for the price. How much would it cost to run your ad in the local paper?

19. BIGGER THINGS

OBJECTIVE: Ap

Write a real estate ad to sell your school building or the White House. Give all the particulars, including the price.

—   —

21. DATELINES AROUND THE WORLD

OBJECTIVE: K, C, Ap

Cut out as many datelines from as many different countries as you can. If the country is not given, be sure to locate it. Using flags or pins, locate these datelines on a world map. What conclusions can you make from these dateline locations? Keep a record from day to day. Graph the daily datelines. At the end of your study, present the data. You might want to do the same activity with only United States datelines. Where are things happening in the United States?

—   —

23. WIRE ME!

OBJECTIVE: Ap, An, S

Check on the Situations Wanted ads. Place an ad as an unemployed ghost. Give your qualifications, salary wanted, etc. Or try one for Tarzan, Dick Tracy, or Scooby-Doo.

20. PET MATH

OBJECTIVE: Ap

Look at the Pets column. What is the average price for pets listed for sale? Compute this answer.

22. CARTOON COMMENTS

OBJECTIVE: An, S

Using news magazines such as Time or Newsweek, collect cartoons which carry a message. Collect several interesting ones and make up questions for your classmates to answer. Example: What has the cartoonist shown? What news event does this relate to? What questions does this pose?

24. HELP WANTED

OBJECTIVE: Ap, An, S

You are a principal with no students. Write a help wanted ad advertising for particular students. What qualifications must they meet? What hours are they needed? Are there job requirements? Pay? What kind of school is this?

25. THE WIRES

OBJECTIVE: K, Ap

Name the two major wire services which provide
national and international news for the local
papers. Explain how a wire service works. Look
for examples of wire service stories. Does one
service have more articles in your paper than
the other?

27. SOCIETY PAGE

OBJECTIVE: Ap, S

Name several different types of articles found
in the society section of the paper. Write an
imaginary wedding announcement for two well
known people. Give the details as you see them
in your paper.
Examples: Superman and Wonder Woman.
         Pinocchio and Little Red Riding Hood.
         King Kong and Bambi
Do you have a picture for your article.

29. VISITORS

OBJECTIVE: Ap, S

A new sports complex has been opened in your
city. Write a society article telling about
10 famous athletes who were there. Interview
them. Include their comments.

26. EDITORIAL CARTOONS

OBJECTIVE: An, S

Examine editorial cartoons in past papers. Write in paragraph form your interpretation of its meaning. Have your class write editorial comments or their interpretation of the cartoon. Compare.

28. SENSATIONAL!

OBJECTIVE: Ap, S, E

You have just had a wing-ding birthday party. It was so sensational that the local paper wrote about and had pictures of it, too. Who was there? Where was it? What did you do? What made it so different? Why was it so special?

30. SPORTS!

OBJECTIVE: K

Find examples on your sports pages of the following:
    wirephoto   tennis article
    soccer article   baseball item
    football item   sports by-line (local)
            sports by-line (syndicated)
List words used to describe the action.

31. SPORTS COVERAGE

OBJECTIVE: K, C

Which sport is getting the most coverage in your paper? What percentage of the stories related to each of the various sports? Can you explain this?

33. BOOK REVIEWS

OBJECTIVE: K

Read book reviews which are written in your paper. Following this style, write a book review of your favorite book or one you have read recently.

35. BOOK SURVEY

OBJECTIVE: An, Ap

Canvas your school or class. Make a list of the top ten books. Publish this list for others to use as a guide. Make a fiction and non-fiction list.

32. FEATURE YOU

OBJECTIVE: An, S, E

A special feature has been written about you because YOU are a superstar in your particular sport. Write it as you would like it to read. What have you accomplished? How did you accomplish this? What does your future hold?

34. REVIEWS AND THE LIBRARY

OBJECTIVE: C

Write book reviews to accompany book displays in your library or learning center. Do these reviews increase the book's circulation?

36. GRAPHING

OBJECTIVE: Ap

Make a bar graph to show circulation of favorite books at your school. Your librarian can help you with this information. Write a news article explaining your data.

37. INTERVIEW-REVIEWS

OBJECTIVE: C

Interview people to gain comments about books to be reviewed. Use this information in book reviews. You may want to include these in your school newspaper.

39. INVERTED PYRAMID

OBJECTIVE: K, Ap, An

Newspaper writing is usually said to be written in the inverted pyramid style. Investigate what this style is like. Find examples in your paper showing this style. Cut them out. Can you find examples which do not fit this style? Cut them out. Give reasons for your selections. Why is the inverted pyramid used by reporters and news writers?

41. IT'S YOUR TURN

OBJECTIVE: Ap, S

Obviously, the headlines in Activity 40 refer to fairy tales and nursery rhymes. Can you think up headlines to accompany other well known tales and rhymes?

38. FAMOUS NEWSPERSON

OBJECTIVE: S

Prepare an original biographical study of a
famous newsperson.

40. IMAGINE THIS!

OBJECTIVE: Ap, S

Using one of the headlines given below, write a
full account of a news release using the in-
verted pyramid style.
"Wolf Wrecks House"
"Glass Slipper Fits"
"Girl Leaves Tuffet"

42. IT'S SENSATIONAL

OBJECTIVE: K, C

Some newspapers are known to use sensational
headlines. What does this mean? Find examples of sensational headlines.

43. WRITE YOUR WONDER STORY

OBJECTIVE: C, S

You are a famous news reporter. Choose a major event in history that you would like to have covered. Write your news story. Include a dateline and by-line.

45. HEADLINES! HEADLINES!

OBJECTIVE: Ap, An

Extra, Extra! Read all about it! Scan the head-lines from the local newspapers. Write down three which really grab you. In several short sentences, speculate on what you think the story will be about. Go back. Read the news story. Did the headline lead you on or was it fairly accurate as a guide to the story?

47. T.V. AND MOVIE REVIEWS

OBJECTIVE: An, E

Read columns in the paper which review movies, theater or T.V. programs. Choose several and point out factual information and phrases which are obviously the opinion of the writer. Does the column appear to be more fact or opinion?

44. INDEX INFO

OBJECTIVE: K

Study the index of several newspapers. What
sections seem to be included in all papers?
What kinds of news are found in each?

46. HEADLINES FROM THE PAST

OBJECTIVE: C, Ap

Write headlines for past events which might
have occurred in local newspapers of the time.
Examples: Franklin Discovers Electricity
          The Civil War Ends
          Lusitania Sinks
Improve on these or choose your own historic
event.

48. DO YOU AGREE?

OBJECTIVE: An, E

Choose the review with which you strongly disagree. Write a letter to this person stating
your beliefs. Quote statements made in the
column with which you find disagreement.
State your facts as well as your opinion.

49. WRITE YOUR OWN

OBJECTIVE: An, E

After analyzing and reading review columns, write
your own review of an entertainment offered in
your community. Again, use facts as well as
opinions.

51. ADVERTISING

OBJECTIVE: C, Ap

Advertising is used to provide money for the
newspaper and is a means of informing the public
about products and services available in the
community. Find different kinds of advertising
in your local paper. Make a collection of ads
that you think are really well done. Estimate
how much of the newspaper is used for advertising.

53. WOULD YOU BUY?

OBJECTIVE: C, Ap, An

Advertising is everywhere. Billions of dollars
yearly are spent to get us, the consumers, to
buy certain products. Try to find examples in
your newspapers for the following advertising
gimmicks:
a. Repetition--repeated phrases or words.
b. Selling words--sometimes patriotic or making
   one feel guilty.
c. Special mood--loved ones, family, nature.

50. COLUMNISTS

OBJECTIVE: An

Compare and contrast <u>local</u> and <u>syndicated</u> columnists.

52. ENRICHMENT PRESS

OBJECTIVE: C, Ap, S

Perhaps you and your classmates will want to work together to put out an edition of Enrichment Press. You will want to include all parts of a regular newspaper.

54. Continued from 53

d. What's new--be the first.
e. Just plain folks--kind grandfatherly
f. Wanting to belong--everyone uses
g. Endorsed by celebrities--Pete Rose says...
h. Statistics--90% use, 1 out of 3 want...

55. GOOD NEWS/BAD NEWS

OBJECTIVE: C, Ap, An

Is it true that what is good for one may be bad
for another? This is an activity which plays
with the opposites, good and bad. There are
several examples to start you thinking. Then,
continue on your own.

---

57. OPINION

OBJECTIVE: An, S, E

We have just received notice from the United
States Department of Education that all schools
in the United States will begin operation on a
six day week, 8:00 to 5:00, 51 weeks of the year.
Only one week will be chosen by each individual
school district. This would be your official
school vacation.

(over)

---

59. FACT AND OPINION

OBJECTIVE: K, An, S, E

Newspapers, magazines and T.V. deal in facts,
but also with opinions. Can you tell the difference? How much of what we read is factual? How
much is opinion? Use the following exercise to
help you. Mark F for fact and O for opinion.

a. The sun can be very hot.
b. Our newspaper is always factual.
c. Spinach is delicious.
d. Joe Namath is a great football player.
e. Teenagers are a wild bunch.

56. Continued from 55

Examples: Good News! My aunt gave me a kitten!
            Bad News! I'm allergic to cats!

            Good News! We're going on a trip!
            Bad News! I get car sick!

            Good News! We have a school holiday!
            Bad News! I have the measles!

58. Continued from 57

It is felt that this is necessary for all students from ages 4 to 18. How do you feel about this? What do you think? Do you have an alternate plan? Do you endorse this plan? Write a letter to your local editor for his "Letters to the Editor" column. Explain your feelings, your needs, and your reaction. Offer alternatives or point out strengths to the above national education system.

60. Continued from 59

f. Kids don't work as hard in school as they used to.
g. Everything on T.V. is educational.
h. Our lakes and streams are polluted.
i. Baby birds actually eat a great deal.
j. That dog is vicious.
k. That was a bad mistake.

Were any of the above statements questionable? Would some need more investigation? Which ones would you question as sometimes fact, sometimes opinion? Is this possible? Find examples in your newspaper of facts, of opinions, of both.

STUDENT INDEPENDENT STUDY PROJECT

Goals: What I hope to learn:

Procedure to follow: Research I intend to do:

   Bibliography:

   Activities I intend to do:

   Materials I need:

Target date for completion: _____

Final Presentation to include:

Student Signature: _____

Teacher Signature: _____

Parent Signature: _____

D.O.K. Publishers

STUDENT WORK LOG

Week I: Mon.
          Tues.
          Wed.
          Thurs.
          Fri.
          Teacher Conference - Needs:
                                Completions:
                                Comments:

Week II: Mon.
          Tues.
          Wed.
          Thurs.
          Fri.
          Teacher Conference - Needs:
                                Completions:
                                Comments:

Week III: Mon.
          Tues.
          Wed.
          Thurs.
          Fri.
          Teacher Conference - Needs:
                                Completions:
                                Comments:

Completion Week

____ Research reports properly written; proofread; rewritte

____ Activities completed.

____ Unit organized.

____ Presentation prepared.

This is a sample form for students' organization of study
skills.

The Teacher Conference is very important on a regular basis
for needs assesment as well as for constant evaluation
and supervision.

88   D.O.K. Publishe